I'm Raybo

Poems

Copyright © Ray Novak, 2013. All rights reserved under International and Pan-American Copyright Conventions. No part of this book may be reproduced or distributed in any form or by any means, or stored in a data base or retrieval system, without written permission from the author. All rights, including electronic, are reserved by the author and publisher.

Printed in the United States of America.

First edition 2013.

Cover photo by Emily Fordyce.

Scurfpea Publishing
P.O. Box 46
Sioux Falls, SD 57101
scurfpeapublishing.com
editor@scurfpeapublishing.com

I'm Raybo

Contents

Introduction by Charles Luden ix
"my saturday morning reasons" 1
decent embers 2
abbo 3
This Land Is 4
Medieval Wheelings 5
stringed beings 6
"For me trying" 7
Kenosha Bound 8
dream meter 10
wedentity 11
Waterside 12
faces 14
hooloonooloopooo 17
Rage 18
En-tropical Disease 20
Miles Away 22
final new year 23
Winter Blue 24
fried raybo 25
skeleton shiver 26
"from the top of this wave" 28
misspelled musing 29
held 30
Stone Circle 31
FARFISA 101 32

hushed	33
i'm softhearted	34
star struck man	35
i don't want	36
Adam and Joy	38
It's All Right	40
lifted	41
Savory	42
Wander The Night	44
Let's Pray	46
The Bed From Which You Rise	48
Footprints	50
nature vs. gadget	52
Abalobadia	53
Mississippi Mud	54
full	56
never gonna happen	57
Flannel Shirt	60
lution	61
peace on the tree	62
"on second thought"	63
seers and beers	64
Quiet Valley Dust	65
"caught an out of service bus"	68
She's Unhealthy	69
color change	70
where i am is everywhere i'm supposed to be	71
"you will see me there tonight"	72
Prophet Nastiness	73
Inspiration	74
yumby	75
Muse	76
Snow Angel	78

"less than what we ask for"	79
"think flecks of silvery tinsel"	80
inches above	81
Some Strange Metaphor	82
What Can I Do	84
stan and geronimo	86
never upon a time	90
"actively fishing for needed inspiration	92
bah bah baby . . . bah bah	93
leader	94
the seven	96
"thoughts dreams and wishes	97
westew	98
Dry Well	99
Skunk Train	100
twenty first	102
welcomer	103
Love's Where You Find It	104
smoke and mirrors	106
present flection	108
who will take you	109
poetry	110
forced fast	111
Soul Time	112
within the next bottomless puddle	113
mirror mirror	114
"music making laughter"	115
first blues in years	116
pico peggy	117
almind	118
"In the way is still involved"	119
a nest in winter	120
rise	121

vii

Introduction
by Charles Luden

    Raybo is a wandering troubadour I met years ago who was wondering about words and the muse. We ended up drinking coffee in cheap cafes and fancy drinks in expensive lounges. While there, on occasion we'd have notebook wars by reading aloud in turn from our steno books of poetic drafts. We ended up on a couple CDs together in the bands *Habitual Groove of It* and *Gypsy Maintenance*. He once stayed at the Chelsea Hotel. I never did. Below is my tribute poem to him from our roving past.
    – July 21, 2013

Nights of the Barking Dog
for Raybo

Be yourself, Ray.
It's OK.
Strum the guitar and howl
to alleviate the pain.
It might go away
even if she doesn't care.
Walking in the night
thinking about the big question.
Oh well. Oh well.

Making up a rhyme
over coffee at the Fryn' Pan
to make her drool drool.
And she's got a short black dress on.
And she's got a white mini dress on.
So wonderful playing pool.
Yes and no are repeated.
Yes and no.
Every now and then the big red car approaches
like a lone rider in a western movie.
Blast! Blast! goes the horn,
and the friends wave,
and the dark haired girl smiles once again.
Once more for Ray
with the strumming guitar.
Then wearing black, you walk away
with a big arm around a small shoulder
into the business end of the night
when normal folks sleep, and
you begin to howl with us old boys
at the Fryn' Pan.
And the beautiful lady by your side
brightens everyone's eyes,
and we too begin to purr that long
cat moan to dawn.
Your red car, Ray.
Your white man power.
Your mystic night.

Charles Luden
August 26, 1991

my saturday morning reasons
for my friday night misses
center around teaching
groups of recovering addicts
how to play on the beach
tactile re-connection
simple beautiful element to offer suffering
vastness of materials
encouragement vs. insistence
impermanence and importanence
symmetrically unique formages
sand castles... you don't need me saying

decent embers

painted bunting
space of stilled moments
where colors touch before blending
sugary shadow
memory of a kiss
dissolved into love unending

abbo

sometimes i get to sleep where angels do their dreaming
to be running wild and screaming
from purest joy
melting my awakening from man to boy
chased into the mischief of the night
beginners light

This Land Is

Well I know we're in a strange spot
I don't know how we ended up here
But for you I'll give it all I got
'Cause you're someone I can trust dear
I don't want to say the same old thing
I know you read me like a book gets
To me you're everything the world could bring
Except the doses we ain't took yet
We just might do this for a long long while
It isn't hard to make it up now
There's no instructions for my lifestyle
I don't believe in being taught how
I just deliver when it really counts
But are the numbers gonna add right
I may not figure when the checks bounce
But I can sing you through a bad night

And I've been to California too
You wouldn't believe the things I found there
But I have always headed back to you
I'm kind of married to the ground here
So it's a circle like it's always been
Who am I to interrupt dear
Could we please just dance around again
I don't know how we ended up here

Medieval Wheelings

Suns rise and ever setting
Suns never go too far away
But sometimes suns are different
And you can't recognize the day

Some suns get lost along the way

I'll stay to grace the morning
I'll stay to have a novelty
Then once we've killed the dawning
Chalk tips to take a poke at me

Love trips can end so foolishly

Some things were never meant to be

Medieval wheels are turning
Old castles topple to the ground
Found faith is ever learning
Found love is faithless to be found

Such things stay uselessly around

Medieval wheels still trace the sound

stringed beings

being useful is the greatest thing to be

being in the way
is still being involved

being what may feel useless at present
may prove invaluable in future availability

being who you really are
is all the moment has you being

bing! bing! bing! bing! bing!

℘

for me trying to separate my romantic gleaning from my poetic exchanges in order to hold face to love's blankness sews a graft that will never take my old heart feeds too many rivers to charge the dams erected against my flow people seldom know what they truly want from an artist but often are quite confident in what they won't allow waving my glass at the sky i toast here's to the unbridled lusty fumbling of the creative heart writhing and sizzling upon the hot sharpened stones of the choosers they will never know what they have missed

Kenosha Bound

In the end of November
So I would remember
I set out to write this song
On a Greyhound from Denver
To Chicago November
Looks awfully cold and long

I remember the springtime
South Padre Island
Where I went for a soft place to fall
For my heart was sure broken
By love's blackened cloak and
The dagger that pierced its wall

When my wife found another
In a man I called brother
All my music turned empty and cold
For I did love them both
As I now love the ghost
Of a marriage not two years old

But I looked towards tomorrow
In a girl drenched in sorrow
Who's sister had recently died
She had come from Kenosha
To heal by the ocean
And for several long days I stayed with her and tried

Ashlee
Ashlee
You're so gentle and free
Won't you lay down your burden
Won't you rest your sweet head
Ashlee
Ashlee
Won't you sing soft to me
Won't you let go of hurting
Let me love you instead

I tried so hard to hide
All my hurting inside
From this beautiful flower now wilting in pain
When she held out her hand
On that sugary sand
Together we found strength to live life again

How the time seemed to fly
When she kissed me good bye
And I watched as she left for an hour or more
Now I'm half a year better
But I can't forget her
That Wisconsin girl on that South Texas shore

Ashlee

dream meter

sheep sleep sagaciously steep tuning times timpani boom-bitty
beep
tap
tap-tippy
flipflopflofleet
savor some singsongy sizz'lin sweet treat sheep
leap feet

wedentity

present
unaccounted for
shipped
but not received
faithful servant
unemployed
runs out of road
learning not to bend the new grass
or kick the stubborn stone
steps on air
then has no feet
stretching for the clouds
arms disappear
gazes at a teardrop
returning no reflection
breathes in all
releases nothing
but a soundless echo
from a sideless stream

Waterside

Amber glow
Where the sunlight meets the mountains' melting snow
Where the tickled water's laughing as she flows
Filtered through the grasses no one even knows
To the flattened stone it's forming far below
Falling towards the spinning earth in raining bow
With far to go

Forrest stream
How I hold you in the highest of esteem
Hidden deep within a maze inside a dream
With your secret sewn inside a muddy seam
Filling into thermal holes exhaling steam
Churning mothers milk from life's immortal cream
We nurse supreme

Waterside
How you call me in and take me for a ride
Waterside

River's edge
I'm beginning to suspect the bet is hedged
As I see them from your belly start to dredge
Redirect you through the tightest little wedge
Empty poisons by the barrel like a pledge
But you may have left us standing on a ledge
We're on a ledge

Ocean blue
I'm afraid we'll have to leave it up to you
With your cleansing and forgiving waters true
My apology is sadly overdue
For the tainted skin upon your primal stew
Now I fear I feel your patience wearing through
We have no clue

I am drawn
To where the water meets the land
If you follow
Step beyond
The fingers made of sand
Waves tomorrow
Dusty dawn
I am guided by your hand
Past the sorrow
Cradle man
In the comfort of your arms

Waterside
How you call me in and take me for a ride
Waterside

faces

we are
so many faces
a crowd within a crowd
but it's only us
it is only us
we honor love by letting go of image
but then there are those faces
they say it all just by hanging there
the emotional road map to our individuality
interstate highway systems constructed by our bloodlines
the signaling tower blazing from our souls
draped like a banner on a loaded set of shoulders
nailed with conviction on the backbone of belief
faces bring us forward to the newness of the day
you can make a face
wear a face
paint a face
share a face
you can kiss a face
miss a face
dis a face
steal a face
shave a face
lick a face
space a face
pinch a face
slap a face
melt a face
bury a face
you can hold your breath 'til your face turns blue
pick a face out of a lineup
put on your best face
forget to tell your face

you can have a face that only a mother could love
one that could stop a clock
or a face like a monkey
a movie star
an angel
you can have an honest face
a face that rings a bell
you can face forward
face off
face up
face east
face time
faceplate
face plant
face lift
turn your face
find your face in the sun
you can face the facts
face the music
face the corner
face your fears
you can face it alone
we can face it together
we can face each other
or be just another face in the crowd
let's face it
you cannot quite put a face to it
stone face
rubber face
scarface
baby face
doll face
clock face

funny face
watch face
clown face
scary face
pizza face
two-faced
defaced
refaced
prefaced
interfaced

shitfaced

face to face
one was said to launch a thousand ships
some people see one on mars
on our moon
countless faces
fill my memory
facing me like my own face in a mirror
i face the future
as i hope to be
a face among so many beautiful faces
not so quickly vanished from the face of this planet
reflecting in the watery eyes
shining from the face of love

hooloonooloopooo

you're lying
you love me
so soon you will show
how you need me
to give you
the love i feel grow
inside our hearts together
such rhythm and flow
you're lying
you love me
i know

Rage

Rage rage you won't win
Rearing back
Fencing me in

No one sees the lines I've drawn
No one knows my rights from wrongs
No one can stand my carrying on the way I do

Higher higher drop me down
Chasing shadows
Across the ground

I shouldn't think some thoughts I think
Shouldn't connect some things I link
Reach out for help before I sink in anger's view

Anger's view
In the fury of the day
Wanting desperately for everything to go another way
But they don't
And she won't
Find the heart to want to stay
Anger's view
Clouding up another day

Over over pictures paint
Colors tolerance grown faint

Blood on boil steaming out
Scream the whisper hush the shout
Loose the grip with grease 'n doubt of what was true

Closer closer to escape
Leave this world
Its troubled gape

I couldn't hurt more once again
Couldn't prevent your master plan
Lost and alone a boyish man in anger's view

Anger's view
In the fury of the day
Wanting desperately for everything to go another way
But they don't
And she won't
Find the heart to want to stay
Anger's view
Clouding up another day

En-tropical Disease

I am a casualty of what I've discovered
The tragedy of an unused gift
The semi-conscious descriptive gaze
And hours of unnoticed public disturbances

In this day of so many purposeless somethings
I am more proud of nothing than anything else

En-tropical disease
Part three
Section four
The wonder years
One of the boys you consumed last summer has struggled to drop me a message
The rind of your heart
The core of your soul
From everywhere the parts go once-eaten

I send clouds

They send me

Some days are soaked
The sogged muddy mind
The scab where I used to think

Here's where I find you
Plugged-in directly to the heartbreak machine
A main vein wire of potent goop
Which slides to the outside of all circumstances

Like a snot-bubbling child, there's no hope for an end
Just growth, annoying development, tumors
Meltdown

And all that is offered
From your sweat-cracked tit-fed worry buddies
Is a banter of fat-rolling chance for removal
To be kept away or not at all
Could it shine a less sensitive light

They're just your friends
They're just your fine
For the crimes of man
And the unapproached fall of nobility

The nightcrawler travels
By consuming what nature provides
Inching its way over the topsoil
To avoid rain-filled holes of bloated death below
This one is hurt by the raindrops now
Transparently spread out
Four times its size
This one is slowly becoming aware

Miles Away

I woke up from a dream this morning
Held you close not knowing
You were so many miles away

Got up, stared out the window
Pulled the shades and hit the pillow
Dreamland is where I'm going to stay

But the sun will shine tomorrow
Brighter than today
Even though the sky is cold and grey

Had to deal with my grievances
Cold water blast to shock my senses
Hey, World, look out it's time to play

Phone rings and I start praying
Wrong number is all it's saying
It's going to be another endless day

But the sun will shine tomorrow
Brighter than today
Even though the sky is cold and grey

I woke up from a dream this morning
Held you close not knowing
You were so many miles away

final new year

nobody thought that we would ever be here
stumbling 'round like it's the final new year's
gathering
you can make it ring
walking in as if you think she'd notice
all the dreams that he's been keeping afloat
still in his eyes
like clouds in skies

winter children are inside in mind to play
coming on like they're coming on some other day
frosted over on a wounded knee to pray
one more fall and they may fly away

if minneapolis ain't too cold to keep you
i'll quit rebuilding your castle in the sand
burn my books in the january bleed through
prairie river you're winding on again

bust ass set her up and watch 'em tumble
weekend pass and it's a touchdown fumble
you fill your roles
who fields your goals
i'll admit i get a little scattered
wind chime mystic wishing wishes mattered
not much you say
make'm anyway

winter children are inside in mind to play
coming on like they're coming on some other day
frosted over on a wounded knee to pray
one more fall and they may fly away

Winter Blue

You looked for me
While I looked for you
We wandered alone
In the fog of the fall
Of the finest winter blue

As I wander through your life again
As I stop to question why
As I stumble through this heartbreak and madness
Until I'm petrified

Strange as it seems
Unreal as it's become
We each had to be
Where we wanted to be
Who knows where we have gone

So you look for me
While I look for you
We wonder alone
In the fog of the fall
Of the finest winter blue

fried raybo

Dear Friends,

So sorry to leave you all in suspended animation for so long. As it is, my latest battle between heart and mind has left me with a bit of a blown fuse and a directionless lack of hope. Everyone has a breaking point and I am most sorry if me reaching mine has left any of you in a tough spot. This is not my intention, but a necessary bi-product of me getting the healthy help out of the darkness I so desperately need. I can't thank you enough for your concern and support. I would do the same for each and every one of you.

I am only allowed limited access to outside communications for awhile, so please forgive my eminent tardiness in response. I will be thinking about and loving you all.

Love,
Raybo

skeleton shiver

skeleton shiver
it's cold
mighty cold
just a thinning bag of bones
to warm your heart
your senses deliver
but never could hold
the blanket of truth you held to start

a walk in this world
raked by darkness and thorn
makes your skin tough
or tattooed with scars
with step after step
many layers get torn
as your blood leaks a map
to where you are
as your blood leaks a map
to who you are

i met you one day
found the sun in your eyes
by the wisdom my mind often seeks
reflecting a picture
of what you could make of me
barnes and noble buddhist
or a music circus freak

oh the games children play
you have seen mine
now show to me
serve me up the most imagined dish
for i want to hold hands
can't you see mine is trembling
reaching for a penny
by a fountain with a wish

still deeper we will go
past the past
past eternity
right up to forever
and nothing
and om
a swim in the stars
that is what my life's meant to be
you see an open door where i see home
you see an open door
where i am home

☙

from the top of this wave
i am above the morning sun reflected in shimmer sand rolling
i am below the fleeing moon turning waters pages past me spilling into
orange and ether laughing
sun, moon, and sea

misspelled musing

here and there...not wanting to feel better
days go by unanswered
bitter and dark
not much solace vs. distraction
cynical laughter and heart hardening
open wings fluttering
pre-destruction windiness
closing me in a resisted trauma hug
repair and recreation
burned in the Godshine
the fleshy stench of disillusion
my insisted-upon dinner companion
nauseous and spent
escaping details
struggle to form a closed story
not close enough
to patch up the hole in my heart sails
awaiting permission to feel good again
wanting a still greyer day

held

feel if you will
an arm around your shoulder
a heartbeat in your ear
be here now
close your eyes

take warmth and heaviness
from calmness breathing
feel the caring of a friend
see the sunshine on a smile
know the memory of a laugh
know that you are known
sacred perfect living soul
loved just for being
with nothing meaning more
no need needing to be
letting everything be right now
for right now
for as long as need be

Stone Circle

Can I meet you in some stone circle
Blinding rays of light
Shine on images of ancient faces
Buried in the night

Will we stand on unnamed ruins
From a time when man could see
More than building stairs to touch the hand
That wrote our destiny

From our cave of amber crystal
Hidden pools of radiance
Harbor silver ships with golden sailors
Stars reflecting dance

We will glide among the tree tops
Where the unpicked flowers grow
From the living will of dying beauty
Crying far below

FARFISA 101

This time we're looking for the real thing

No I'm not paid real well for the work I'm in
And I don't work too hard for the things I own
Sometimes I think real hard about the way I sin
Sometimes I slip into the comfort zone
I slip
Into the comfort zone

hushed

what does she see
staring from the snow angel
what secrets do the snowflakes whisper
who draws the breath
frozen cloud steamed within her
snoring in the paling sky of winter

i'm softhearted
wanting to talk it out
on a pile of expressions
smaller than i look
more confident than i'd realized
within the strengthless fall
crying love

star struck man

this fire is slowly a dier
the curtain of night folded in
hold me closer fasten us tighter
to the twinkles of a starstruck man

it is a cold long wait till the morning
feel these shivers gripped hold of my hand
time's a smolder'n heart in the sunrise
on the ashes of a starstruck man

i've been hit by the best
lonely long drawn out test
i scream up to the frozen milkyway
from this caustic cosmic shore lit
by your crashing comet orbit
ignite my night in splendid streaks of day

i was just walking out on the planet
dodging low-flying clouds with my habits
dragging deep-seeded dreams from atlantis
to the banks of an unexplained source

but this ground will stay warm through the daytime
you will quiet my need to explain
that to rekindle hearts takes a windstorm
or a cinder from a starstruck man

i don't want

i don't want
what i want
i don't want to want
i've no time
far as i can see neither does anyone

i'm so tired
of what i'm tired of
i just want to love the whole damn thing
rest my weary quest upon your offering

is this the start of a journey
or the end of the line
will you satisfy your own needs
while i'm out here ducking mine

i'm so sorry
being sorry
for the sorry me i am and could be
could be being me is beyond apology

i let loose
of what i'm loose of
let me loose the lonely loss i've found
left amidst the lost you find in everytown

and i touch touch
like i fear fear
i listen hard to what i hear
i see the sights
i sight the seas
whose flooding flood washed over me
set me free

so i don't want
what i want
i don't want to want
i've no time
all i have is time
time is all i've ever had to keep me here

i long to be
a being being
to sing the song
a singer sings
to live the life
to love the love
i'm sure the maker made us of
up up above

Adam and Joy

Please let me take you with me on a train ride
To the woods where we can pick some wild mushrooms
After sunset they'll be cooking with sweet grasses
On a campfire that took so long to get started
In this crevice we have packed our warm and dry
Like this blanket we have spread out on the ground here
No you didn't see me when I picked this flower
And you placed it in your hair like you're a goddess
We are dancing to the music that our souls make
As the smell of smoke is hanging in our clothing
Your fingers play the drum along with nature
The scary stories keep us up for hours
Inside the sleeping bags we've zipped together
The flashlight that you used to make your cheeks glow
Then showed me all the bones inside your fingers
Ran screaming from a bug into the rain
But you don't mind me laughing while I hold you
Because you ate all the chocolate for the smores girl
It's fun to watch your face when you've been naughty

To think of what you looked like as a baby
If you were tickled 'till you ran your breath short
Or someone made you smile when you were pouting
Now warm your hands around this cup of green tea
I'll wrap this blanket gently 'round your shoulders
To sit with you in stillness by the fire
You'll be awake for hours from the sugar
But somewhere in the rhythm of the forest
A lullaby is croaking from a frog pond
And I can feel your weight upon my body
Yet can't believe you smile while you are sleeping
Slowly I will lift you in a cradle
Then carry you back over to the bedroll
In hopes that you've forgotten 'bout the bug there
Thinking how I'm going to make you breakfast
If I can keep the fire lit 'till morning
But who could leave the warmness of your cuddle
We'll end up driving into town to Denny's
To frighten all the people who've had showers
And tangled in your hair I see the flowers
I wonder if you still can feel the flowers

It's All Right

It's all right by me
It's all right by me

If I leave myself alone again tomorrow
Teach my soul the final way
Become the distance found between the things I borrow
Life's not wasted on today

But even now
I travel on and on
I search for help along the way
Because even now
With everything gone wrong
I live to learn to look the other way

If I find a way to drift along to you love
If you've waited there for me
Then may the road become the dreams we are made of
May my song speak soft to thee
May the world know we are of the kind
To give and take in harmony
Because even now
With heaven's will aligned
Our love is something only yet to be

It's all right

lifted

star of my heart sky, to see your grace in my mind's eye, dancing atop reflected sun on crystal waves, insisting i raise my own tattered freedom flag higher still to stronger charging winds of great adventure . . . beloved, i am yours upon either of these shores and as many undiscovered as you'll have my hand in yours. you who harvest sweet passions from the world and set them loose where they should be; further, adrift, and ever free. take me.

Savory

Short
Sweet
Tall
Cool
Trailed by a back beat
Hidden like a jewel
An interconnection of style and grace
Some bartered collection
Of singular space
One whole
One all
One passionate play
One view of tomorrow
From duality's day
For the sun sees the moon
As ahead
As behind
As the voice of a tune
Resurrects the divine
Vine, vine
How the souls intertwine
As the voice of a tune
Resurrects the divine

You
Me
Here
There
Reaching for a heartbeat
Drawing in the air
An echoing story
Of soul meeting soul
Impersonal glory
Restringing the bow
Big guns
Big news
Big smallness today
Big views from the monsters
That haul us away
How I feel so alone
Face to face with the crowd
There's so few of us left
Here for crying out loud
Loud, loud
We are crying out loud
With so few of us left
Here for crying out loud

Wander The Night

I'm not quite sure what's coming
Through this open funnel swirling
Down to my place on this ground
They've been reaching out forever
Like a dream of heaven's fingers
With a spirit moaning sound
When the grass bends painter's circles
To the earth and rocks in purple
Underneath the fading light
And the ground behind you rumbles
With the naked feet of children
Wishing stars to kiss the sky goodnight

Oh the night

You'd wander the night were it not for sleep
You'd follow your instincts and run too deep
In an endless display of the plans you keep
To the ground
Near the sky
On your feet

It's an antique understanding
Of the way things used to be
How a floatless water landing's
In the future we can see
When you're young enough to realize
You're old enough to leave

On a clear day you see only more
Of what you know so well
And it's clouding up the distance
Of tomorrow's waking spell
So you send your bones to work again
You send your mind to play
You send your heart to anyone
Send your soul to pray

You'd wander the night were it not for sleep
You'd follow your instincts and run too deep
In an endless display of the plans you keep
To the ground
Near the sky
On your feet

Let's Pray

Let's pray you don't pollute me
For noticing things that you may never see
You did not have to loose me
On the troubled shores of your mind

Your message sounds so frightening
Engulfed by the land and enraged by the sea
Both slightly more enlightening
Than the thoughts you are sharing with me

You'll want to
You'll want to
You'll never leave home
Because you'll never be lonely there
If the elements haunt you
And taunt you to roam
They can carry you soft
Through the air

Heaven knows why
Angels fall from the sky
While we're waiting
Waiting
Harvest comes late
While the world cultivates
All this waiting
Waiting

You'll want to
You'll want to
You'll never leave home
Because you'll never be lonely there
If the elements haunt you
And taunt you to roam
They can carry you soft
Through the air

Raybo

The Bed From Which You Rise

When you find
That central buzz
Troubles wisdoms
Under coil
Take concern
Towards who you judge
Lest you taste
A common spoil

Lonesome words
Ring out of me
They seek to find
Your harmony
Awoken dreamers
Close your eyes
Know well the bed
From which you rise

Cold hollow heart
To hide inside
Left all alone
A frightened child
Just change your road
Enjoy the ride
Flowers and weeds
Are growing wild

Hard comfort sails
A rocky sea
Drowning the ones
That will not be
Poor helpless fools
Old selfish pain
The more you list
The more you wane

Footprints

Ogalala
Quiet water
I have seen your massive prairie growing wild
From the Pinto
Palomino
Where the sunshine fills the grasses three feet high
Stood to wonder
Lost in faces
As my questions rise alone and opened wide
Mystic brother
Calm my worry
Hear this traveler give a warrior's thunder cry

Hee-ee-eeoo
Thank you earth for the footprints that I leave
Hee-ee-eeoo
Thank you sky for the home I will receive
Hee-ee-eeoo
Thank you water for the blankets that you weave
Hee-ee-eeoo
Thank you fire for the spirit of the magic I believe

Minnehaha
Laughing water
Have you let the light you're made of slip away
Once the trickster
Now your sister
Will your children know the night you've left was day
Farmer telling
What are you selling
Your fields go to seed and unmown hay
Distant singing
Slips nature's clinging
As if money were the highest price to pay

Hee-ee-eeoo
Thank you earth for the footprints that I leave
Hee-ee-eeoo
Thank you sky for the home I will receive
Hee-ee-eeoo
Thank you water for the blankets that you weave
Hee-ee-eeoo
Thank you fire for the spirit of the magic I believe

nature vs. gadget

last night
in the yard
i shined a green laser
at the green glowing ass
of an airborne lightning bug

the results were illuminating

Abalobadia

Abalobadia
Fragrant corner
Nestled in the woods
You're off the coastal highway
California
Sure are looking good
You bring a lot of people
To your message
Like I know you should
Oh Abalobadia
Tell your secrets
To your brotherhood

Aaahaahaa!
In the early morning sun
Aaahaahaa!
Welcomed in when work is done

The fraternity
Of living free
Your name is like a poem

Abalobadia
On that twisting road
Back home

Mississippi Mud

Mississippi mud
Knocking at your door
You can hear the thud
As you're falling to the floor
Water's getting high
Like it's never been before
In the streets of New Orleans
She can't take anymore

Levy's gonna break down
Did you hear a strange sound
There's a bumper chute floating like a wet frown
And a small girl standing in her night gown
Reaching for a swept away . . .
Another life line
Hanging from the grape vine
Have to find another place to get a shoe shine
So there's not as many standing in the lunch line
What's another suburb anyway

Raise another glass
Have another round
Safe inside the mask
Out to paint the town
Secrets buried deep
Graves above the ground
Be careful what you keep
When the rain's falling down

Levy's gonna break down
Should we head for high ground
Is there time to make a call to tell the brown town
But we gotta save the room to fit the gold crown
Handed down from yesterday
They never knew us
What's with all the big fuss
Should we call another vote upon the brain trust
Time to paint another coat over the old rust
What's another suburb anyway

full

some
how
or
another
from
one
less
likely
grew
many
most
fine
full
of
joy

never gonna happen

there's just no use explaining
all the trouble
all the paining
i get
heading
where
i am aiming
i keep happening to me
gradually
there is a picture
lost romantic
in its nature
inexplicit nomenclature
roaming free
roaming free

i'm in love
with a never-gonna-happen
i can hear them up there laughin'
from their know-it-all perch
calling out favors
just to see what i've been missing
just a taste of what i'm dishing
to the world
to the world

maybe i'll write a song
about the long road between
finding every word i mean
under acres of jewels

maybe i'll write a song

about taking a vacation
from the self depreciation
of a fool
of a fool

i'm in love
with a shouldn't-even-go-there
you can see it's going nowhere
up the vanishing rope
who decides
when hits collide
shattered wholeness
into thin air
pulling rabbits from your hat hair
using mirrors and smoke

maybe i'll spend my time
teaching angels about dancing
across the surface of a stick pin
in the bare foot of freedom

or should i waste my time
teaching bees about the honey
let the birds nest up my money
while my face
awaits its season

to be loved

i'm in love

with a hurry-up-and-happen
i'm around the bend from snapping
from the wait
love
from the wait
don't be late
i'll miss my turn
i've been spinning 'round forever
the direction of the weather
is all i learn
all i learn

maybe i'll live a life
in service to all mighty
just the two of us all tidy
amidst all of this sin

brethren
i'll live my life
without such singular relations
with a massive allocation
of close friends
closest friends

Flannel Shirt

Thinking about putting on a flannel shirt
Seems like the wintertime's always gotta hurt
No matter where you live
No matter how warm
You're paying for your summer
In the middle of an icy storm

Some people come home
Some people stay away
Some people won't travel
When the weather turns grey
But there's stories to be told
There's babies passed around
There's my tears falling on a grave
In the cold, cold ground

How much time
Until we pass this way again
Seems like I'm never gonna make new friends
Never have the money or the time to spend

You were on my mind
Since we met
Until the end
We didn't let it break
But we had to learn to bend
I'm never going to not miss you again

lution

there
where strength pauses
a fall
only forgiveness will outlast shame
from mis-connected wanting
from slow-growing hearts
nested deep in bony branches
not sleeping

peace on the tree

attempted profile, diagnosis, and remedy questionnaire

unnumbered

is it a good feeling...running others down?
does it make you the kind of man you deserve to be?

who rides your bus?
are all your stops of schedule and necessity, void of
mystery and chance?

is being unreachable by some payment enough to keep
you where you are in your place?

is the falseness in your heart but a whisper that
you can not stop listening for?

cruelty is the tool of continuance

you have, do, and will eat your own

on second thought
maybe my mind shouldn't be used
for wrapping around anything

seers and beers

may you come to know the sweetest and subtlest of
flavors on your path towards pathlessness. it is all
as is should be, perfect in its shortcomings. we are
blinded by both bright light and heavy darkness,
needing only to see that we don't need to see to see.
see?

Quiet Valley Dust

I took a shower
In San Antonio
To wash off that Kerrville dust
I lost three shades
From my suntan
My girl lost a cup size from her bust
It's a strange
Return to strangers
I've a hard time giving up the trust
Of those three weeks
Escape from anger
Smiles swallowing the Quiet Valley dust

Once on a darkened winter mountain top
I waded through the snow up to my knees
I saw the world made up of rolling rocks
As I gazed above to see the Leonids
Shooting stars
I can't begin to count
Sent tearing through the nighttime's blackened hue
And I followed every single line
Wishing time and time again for love from you

Glitter dome
Shimmer globe
Wind's sparkling sea
We're forever under graces
We may never even see
Catching stars
Filling hearts
Letting be
While we're out here on the planet being free

Crowned by autumn's final falling
There was mercy with your tender hand in mine
To the lake we sent love's calling
In the gentle wind the sun warmed our reply
Heart to heart
We shared our secrecy
Pausing long enough to laugh at asking why
And you rocked me in your decency
When you sang to me the sweetest lullaby

Magic words
Softer voices
Harmony
We were waiting for a message
When the lake turned into sea
Thankful hearts
Kindred souls
Mystery
While we're out here on the planet being free

So I left you there in Austin
With a hand
In your hand
Where my hand used to be
I have thought about the loss and
How it takes so damn long getting back to being me
But you say you'll be returning
When the river's reached the bridge
Where the land forms from the sea
Now I'm all alone in Texas
Trying hard to meet the cost upon the price of being free

Don't take that shower
In San Antonio
Don't wash off that Kerrville dust
Let your skin glow in the sunshine
Lose your girlfriend your job and every buck
It's a strange return to strangers
I've a hard time giving up the trust
Of those three weeks
Escape from anger
Smiles swallowing the Quiet Valley dust

caught an out of service bus
to not a through street

She's Unhealthy

Style

We'll just say there's nothing left to save
You turn too fast
You spin yourself into an early grave

She's unhealthy
Won't you take a look at how she lives
She's not welcome anywhere I've been
When you're not listening
She absolves herself of all your sins
She's not welcome anywhere I've been

Box yourself inside futility
Bump into the walls
Inside your own senility

She's unhealthy
Won't you take a look at how she lives
She's not welcome anywhere I've been
When you're not listening
She absolves herself of all your sins
She's not welcome anywhere I've been

Oh the damages rendered for payments lost
You're still within a knife's throw my little swan

color change

bend a tree wind
striped novembering sand
butterfly hover by
doors opened in
breathed away
painted thin

subject line:
where i am is everywhere i'm supposed to be

i am a high-functioning volunteer
an american disability
unrecognized
maybe it is an ugly word
vicious letter v
then all the un-ing and crying
perhaps i could petition for better parking
but i gave away my car

you will see me there tonight
seek between the flipping clips
free the flimsy flossy film
clear corrosive cloudy layers
glean a glisten from a glance
or gaze up and to the right
tonight
all swirly

Prophet Nastiness

Don't you be my friend
Nothing's left to lend
Sympathy's not mine to offer
Stay away from me
Keep your flattery
Can't stand to waste my talents on the blasphemy of youth

Distance has its price
My mind will suffice
Take it now or never bother
Wisdom takes no time
All you have is mine
I'll make more to feed the hungry as they give their food away

Wicked dreams I've had
'Bout my mom and dad
How they held no other purpose
I've been raised to see
Nothing's more than me
Criticism takes no refuge from my cynical displays
Arm yourself or die
Be as good as I
Or you'll end up being nothing
Try to settle back and hey
I'll consume your slack and hey
By the looks of things you can't afford to give up any more

Inspiration

I wait for inspiration to be coming into
I wait for inspiration to be coming into
I wait for inspiration to be coming into me

I'm alive and I know it
I'll tell you so
I have died on the side
Of your burning shore
You know I don't mind knowing
I don't know more than you
You're so fine and you're so pretty
I have sunk to the depths of your sunken city
I will brave every wave in this sea of pity

I wait for inspiration to be coming into
I wait for inspiration to be coming into
I wait for inspiration to be coming into me

I sit alone on the Gulf of Mexico
I nearly drown to the sound of your driving soul
You know I don't mind opening another door to you
You're so strong and you're so endless
I'm so weak and small and friendless
I have sung my song 'till I've lost my senses

yumby

forty-something me
wants to tell thirty-something me
how right i was about the twenty-something me

Muse

O muse I have found you
Come to call you my sister
Saw the angels surround you
Saw the road start to blister
Felt these wall start to crumble
From the strength of your beauty
Can't believe I'm still standing on this ground

Sacred heart soaked in wisdom
Bleeds like tears through the window
Fly like doves in a rain storm
Burst in flames from this shadow
How I hunger to hear you
Reach these ears with your voice
There's so much heavy silence in this sound
In this sound

Have I found my passage
To that sky over yonder
Have I found my way uptown
Blessed muse you've delivered
From the roads I have wandered
Didn't know which way was up 'till you came down
You came down

Shining sun I have seen you
Rise from deep in her waters
Take today by the reigns
Lead this dance with your daughters
Stumbling forth on your beaches
Draw the souls bound to reach you
As you drift through the river of the sky
Of the sky

Mirrored soul I have seen you
I have known you forever
We have drowned in your oceans
We have fried in your deserts
Break this hold now I dare you
Grown strong from the ages
Is it light that's reflecting in your eye
In your eye

Have I found my passage
To that sky over yonder
Have I found my way uptown
Blessed muse you've delivered
From the roads I have wandered
Didn't know which way was up 'till you came down
You came down

Snow Angel

We'll be reading from the book of sin

I hurt myself
In front of friends
So they all see
There's nothing good left here inside of me
I follow through
Down to the soul
There's nothing worse
Than rot . . . rot and roll

The one-armed motorcycle man has but one trick
He rides around in circles
Until he's sick
He's not you
So you're alright
So hang about
Until the light
The light

The temperature is dropping
I'm cooling down
The pop cycle of life
I do my earthly carvings
On hallowed grounds
The pop cycle of life
I'm freezing

less than what we ask for
will take more than we can make

☙

thin flecks of silvery tinsel
fly in from everywhere
forming sheer sheets of dust
liquifying as design is believed
shaping, becoming
or questioned, scattered
vulnerable as a stack of crumbs
drying in a relentless breeze

inches above

hot, bliss-filled, stony, sandy summer here. here
here! over-hearing from the new links, undoubtedly
missing some of the past. but this moment....oooh the
taste of tasting a single flavor! in a lick i hear the
downhill slide of a jazz organ solo, a hammer swung, a
turning wave, and some sea beasts. i can smell
jasmine and flavored fires finding their meals, aloft
in the begging breeze, on its knees, for another
relentless day fry, then, goodbye, colored sky, full
of saharan sands, tomorrows, shadows.

Some Strange Metaphor

Welcome to your town
Hope you follow through
Tried all that I could taste
Now I leave it up to you

Waiting for the train
Guess where I should stand
Are we overboard
Is this promised land

I've got more than you
You see more than me
Some things never change
Some things will never get to be

Windows up above
Tunnel under ground
Those who say they love
Consummate the sound

I should have known by now
This would happen
I couldn't wait for more
Some strange metaphor

Not so long ago
When you look back into your mind
Not so long a road
When it's stretched out for your eyes

You said nothing to me
You said nothing of the kind
You said nothing to me
You said nothing of the kind

To you
The book of kind

Welcome to your town
Hope you follow through
Tried all that I could taste
Now I leave it up to you

Waiting for the train
Guess where I should stand
Are we overboard
Is this promised land

Is this promised land

What Can I Do

Lend a hand
Guide the way
Take a stand
Seize the day
Lift a heart
Tell the truth
Learn from elders
Learn from youths
Build a temple
Plant a seed
Sense a purpose
Fill a need
Rest an anger
Heal a wound
Raise a spirit
Howl a moon
Find a lover
Stand alone
Love your Mother

Welcome Home
Rock your baby
Flip your lid
Light a candle
Up the bid
Fight injustice
Make your peace
Hold on tight
Be released
Climb the highest
Take the plunge
Clear the cobwebs
Set the sun
Sing your praises
Harmonize
Trust your instincts
Spot the lies
Wish tomorrow
Live today
Let the whole bunch of balloons just drift away

stan and geronimo

he met her out at burning man
on a pair of stilts
in the desert sand
she was painted up
from the waist on down
while her top was golden tan
she was eating fire as the sun sank low
when she waved him in
and they shared a bowl
she explained her name was geronimo
he said his name was stan

they kept by the fire
and they kept real high
where they whispered and laughed
as the freaks strolled by
she said no one here
is as strange as i
stan said he was a government chemist
she had followed each road
that her heart beat on
he paid student loans
and lived with his mom
she's felt a little lost
since the dead's been gone
he had three credits left to be a dentist

she had always found a home
with the rock and rollers
he had never left home
was a pretty good bowler
she had vampire fangs
to his pearly white molars
who'd be thinking they'd be singing such a song
he was very well insured
but he never took a chance
she could earn good drugs and money
from adult exotic dance
together it could never
be a typical romance
just some boobs
and the moon
and a bong

she had caught vd
from an exchange student kid
with a sweet german smile
and a bump on his lip
she would never want to spread it
but she figured that she did
in the 80's everybody was infected
he once saved a little money
from a newspaper route
bought some orthopedic shoes
that had left him with the gout
but he read a lot of pamphlets
so there wasn't any doubt
he still checked in twice a year to be inspected

she would never own more
than she could carry when she'd walk
he had every childhood toy
many still in the box
he was just a little boy
she's as old as the rocks
and could carve a man to pieces with her knife
she could step into the shadows
then just disappear completely
take a shower out in public
in a fountain indiscreetly
she had never met a stranger
that she didn't want to meet
he had never done his laundry in his life

they could never find a reason
far too steep
and so they stepped
they never found a reason
not to leap
so they leapt
thinking nothing worth the keeping
is a thing that should be kept
they just started
where their hearts would let them go
he shared a little comfort
she shared a little pain
and they shared some body fluids
then a shower in the rain
the crazy group of crazies
thought themselves a bit more sane
every time they heard him scream
geronimo!

they made love that night
perfect strangers without guilt
sometimes rolling on the ground
sometimes high up on the stilts
he had felt a bit deflowered
but he didn't let it wilt
she felt pretty
in the gritty desert dawn
when the festival was over
they thought what's the use pretending
is there anything worth starting
that departing isn't ending
several feet above the people
through the crowd she left descending
he watched her
in an hour
she was gone

they could never find a reason
far too steep
and so they stepped
they never found a reason
not to leap
so they leapt
thinking nothing worth the keeping
is a thing that should be kept
they just started
where their hearts would let them go
he shared a little comfort
she shared a little pain
and they shared some body fluids
then a shower in the rain
the crazy group of crazies
thought themselves a bit more sane
every time they heard him scream
geronimo!

never upon a time

i don't know what it is
getting stranded like this
trying to hook an old loop to a new hall
putting notion to words
for the love of a girl
that had never started happening at all

she can't help but kill you
you can't help but die
there's some truth to be had in between
"how we don't reach enough for the people we care for"
"how we don't even know what we mean"

but i love you
sweet angel
in a vast folded blanket
as secure as it's sacred
draped on frozen belief
we can meet in the middle
surfing folds of forgiveness
through this thread-barren fabric
we are naked beneath

there's a feather adrift on the wind
there's a being where there never had been

i am written by my poetry
could never word it out of me
growing in the soils of scattered gardens
dreams embrace the pleasure
lesser hearts would burst the pressure
building in my basement's shattered bargains

she can't help but kill you
you can't help but die
love can only surrender to time
when we find we have been in a circling wind
when we find we're much more than we find

please believe me
sweet angel
i could never leave you stranded
out wherever we have landed
far from faith's house of cards
may we find out when it's finished
we are closer to beginning
the happiest of endings that a tragedy could start

there's a feather adrift on the wind
there's a being where there never had been
there's an icicle melting to rain
there's a never and never again

actively fishing for needed inspiration
willingly offering an equal exchange
many moments being lived
within the fractured flow
hard times
soft livers
striving to change as much as stays the same
to notice as much as must pass by

why?

bah bah baby . . . bah bah

when i finally woke up
they had taken it away
the purist white smiles hit the paper
we're winning
god loves us
the captions all say
with our cause
we are everyone's saviors

but i've stood by those dumpsters
of medical waste
past the line
of your vulgar sign-waving
where i've seen total strangers
scream into the face
of the growing-up kids
they're there saving

we all have opinions
some are beaten to death
some will fight
to make right
of our living
'till there's no governed choice
but to swallow the voice
of opinions that just keep on giving

so we follow the herd
this compassion of man
we pretend that it's not getting hotter
with distortions of words
even god's favorite lambs
know not but the way to their slaughter

leader

you are the leader
of the whole free world
placed there by money
and power
and grace
you have agendas
big favors to repay
the forces that figure
your head for this space

will history name you
the son of your father
or simply remember the wars you have waged
a tall pile of ashes
enduring our freedom
while building a stronger and shinier cage

all filled with rage

you have landed on water
ensconced in america
filling the mirror of pride with your flexes
slurping the bottom
of earth's mother's kettle
while blowing a hole in the world
shaped like texas

we're rowing faster
the ground's getting nearer
like the harder we hit
then the deeper we'll be
you've let loose the war pig
you criminal bastards
it's time we repaint the flag
blue red and green

it seems white's just too damn clean

the seven

and it rains and it rains like flypaper magic maddening tragic
somethings you just know never told so far aloft reflection
one from one one from one one from from simple begets original
shadow of god shadow of God shadow of of
all looks to none as the favorite sun
born from mother nothingness
who was fucked to begin with

thoughts dreams and wishes
echo around
bouncing in a big black cave
elusive inspiration
grows enchanted by the sound
of what a soul with nothing
fights to save
just these thoughts
these dreams
these wishes
lonely soul creating now
thinking
dreaming
wishing for what's meant to be
and for what has happened
to serve some purpose somehow

westew

trying to eliminate the word is
quite the difficult thing to do
leaving you with maybe at best
awareness is probability patterns
on a certain level we are the same
experience for experience
non-simultaneously experienced
perspective is limited by its faith
belief systems need moderation
best not to completely believe
in yours or anyone else's
trouble for any particular science
yet true to the nature of life

Dry Well

Sometimes there's a rhythm
Flowing softly from the earth
If you're navigating freely
Win or lose
You'll know exactly what you're
Worth . . . less information's
Come to cloud my by and by
Yet I'll try to be the trusting one
The day the well runs dry
Well I'll try to be the trusting one
The day the well runs dry

So you propagate the image of a sinner
And you propagate the image of a saint
You tangle with the matters of illusion
You try to find a home for all the pain
For the beat you are not sure of travels faster
Than the underlying rumble of belief
Are we turning down a world we haven't lived in
Are we closer to the spelling of relief

On and on I'm only left with
What I'd feel like
If I woke and you were gone

Skunk Train

Rolling rolling rolling
Train it keeps a rolling
And it's going to the one place I can't ride to
Skunk train
Skunk train
Don't you know you've left your baby far behind you

Glory glory glory
You've found your favorite story
Now the answers all can fall into alignment
Skunk train
Skunk train
Can't you see it's not your space it's your confinement

There's a railway line that runs
Through the redwoods of the north
Where the mighty Skunk train chugs
To the wide Pacific shore
But you're going back to find
What I've had to leave before
Skunk train I can't hear you anymore

Trying trying trying
So many miles a crying
And they haven't brought the cart 'round for some time now
Skunk train
Skunk train
Hurry back before my heart leaks all the kind out

Farther farther farther
Why should we even bother
To derail this coming hell on the horizon
Skunk train
Skunk train
There's much more to see than people put their eyes on

twenty first

full on psychedelic solstice
one minute in the love light
next minute flung into writhing darkness
pasted to my ludoviko brainpan like a culture-starving teen
being open for hosting both sides of the emotional swing
leaves me slightly blissful
with heavy hierarchical visions

i wanted to send you the verse i wrote in the dark at 3:33am
because you are the threes reflected beyond time
and embody the spirit of many sacred raybo wishes
infinite is the first breath of truth
we cry because we breeze right through it
passing right over important fractions of life not included
a word fits a moment like a loss of importance
larger grows the clutter of was

welcomer

stream of life handler
ready decider
softly-wrapped firmness
entrusted space provider
calming love from fear
coaxing strength from strain
newness and experience
again and again and again
such stars and comets
such regally loyal beliefs
what marvel held for profession
what crisis can come from release
how fortunate slides the body
to such beautiful hands as those
to know on the first waking moment
love can catch you from falling alone

i thank you

Love's Where You Find It

I fell in love one night
At Suds City
She was wearing checkered biking pants and
Looking pretty
Just pumping quarters in a washer
That was broken
So I strolled on over and said
Wouldn't you like to spin your load with me
You can use up all my Oxydol and I'll still stay cling free
No I didn't catch your name
But I bet that it's Blair
Hell, I'm not psychic
I can see it written on your underwear

I fell in love one night
At Sam's Deli
She was molesting cold cuts that were old and
Ripe and smelly
Sort of looking sexy as she fingered
Through the cattle
So I stepped in closer and my
Tongue began to rattle
Wouldn't you like to salt your pork with me
You can case up all my sausage
Make me ten percent fat free
No I didn't see the ring
I bet he's cheap and mean
Hell, I'm no counselor
It's just true love never turns your fingers green

Oh
Love's where you find it
It can grow on every tree

Oh
There's no easy way to hide it
Could be there for you
You
You
But is it there for me

I fell in love at Denny's
Breakfast in my jammies
She was taking orders
I had *moons over my hammy*
Sort of looking slinky as she softly beat my egg whites
So I stepped in closer
Just to ask perhaps if she might
She might
She might
Might you want to split the bill with me
You could butter up my home fries
Toss me toothpicks as I leave
No, I didn't see the scars
I bet that really smarts
The age old story
You can change your sex
You'll never change your heart

Oh
Love's where you find it
It can grow on every tree
Oh
There's no easy way to hide it
Could be there for you
You
You
But is it there for me

smoke and mirrors

your magic wand is circling
a smoky ring
ten billion restless souls
await your conjuring
will you liken to a mirror
reawaken sleeping fear
will you somehow stir the secrets of this recipe
into the baking brick of our democracy

your faker's sleeve has ridden up
a dying hand
the trap door latch is trembling
beneath your stand
how you open says-to-me
we believe our fantasy
revealing what the box seats all have paid to see
the lady sawed in two was our democracy

where you are at now is where i used to be
there was no one here left to point the right to me
where we were before is where we are again
havers have the haves like haves have always been

ride her hard she's dying like
a twisted trick
the emerald city counted
every golden brick
don quixote stands alone
like a stranded traffic cone
between the superhighway and eternity

for a limited engagement
our democracy

behind the smoke and mirrors
greased machinery making fears

present flection

when we first met
i wasn't sure if you wanted to be my friend
so i tried to trick you into it
figured you'd eventually bring 'round some of your real friends
maybe kick my ass or something
but hey, at least i'd be out there with the cool kids
i knew not what to do once the rumble didn't happen
had to start making shit up just to see how far you'd go
which is exactly where we've been for all these years now
me playing you for the chump that you most certainly are
fucking rube

who will take you

could only a mother?
even she didn't always want you around
like that time when she was naked
or whenever you were covered in shit and poverty

to love is to have other things going on

poetry

if the sadness of my poetry
could draw you in
to comfort me
i need not write
another word
to show you how
i reel and hurt
if sounding out
each syllable
would make your heart fill overfull
then scarcely would i need to find
a partner to complete my rhyme
no need to seek
the perfect way
so say the words
i need to say
you'd calm my brow
to quiet me
were you to feel
my poetry

forced fast

pouring my heart
on the hot rocks
cooks like meat
sizzling
browning
waiting to be flipped
seasoned with hope
this thyme might be different
dressed well and tender
my own mouth watering
starving to sample said savory sauce
full from a gut kick appetizer
my pinkness is blackened
well done
no such thing as a table for one

Soul Time

Well it's soul time, the whole time
These weddings and funerals
Where we all gain and lose a friend
It's like the sunshine, a hard climb
As I see their faces
How I wish it would never end

I go to parties where I can't stand the sound
Of the voices and spaces where you're not around
Doors that swing open again and again
Why can't it be you walking in

We're all part of something that's not meant to hold
Like the ocean warm, a thunderstorm, or doing what you're told
Stumbling and dancing 'till the daylight is seen
Making up for the lonesome between

That's where you'll see them when life's swinging low
All the death-broken people who cannot let go
Won't you give them your comfort won't you empty your hand
Life is just sharing what we don't understand

I'll write, we'll call you, please stop when you're near
Let's try and do this the same time next year
I'm guided to you by a star up above
So willing to find you here lost in my love

within the next bottomless puddle

to the extent
that earth still clings to feet
where stubborn wishes meet
beneath old fishes creek
in upside-down mystique
some children wish for you
some lamp rub big to-do
where from your knowing cloud
enchantments spoke aloud
get wasted 1..2..3..
before they set you free

before they set you free
loose with your magic ways
locked up dark so many days
cause now to spout deserved wrath
split bright 'n wide the splendid path
towards this journeys sacred end
back in your magic lamp again

mirror mirror

..........present during transformations
portals lit in swirling heartglow
pulsing channel radiations
spun into the everthrough
breathed into the everflow.............

music making laughter
your eyes across a dancing fire
big dose of betterness medicine
iz is pining for a very real
february sort of way

first blues in years

doing the time
out of rhythm with care
spun through to done
tumbled back down each stair
power less
what a mess
only darkness coming through
power less over you

pico peggy

way out on the resaca
lives a girl selling tacos
to the men who work on the steel line
for an extra two quarters
she will fill up their orders
with the grace of her garden
soaked in lime

well they call her pico peggy
she's so tall dark and leggy
she chops those home-grown veggies every day
she's just north of the border
but when you lay down your quarters
you'll be pining for the hills of monterey

in a little wind-blown shack
with the mixed-matched chairs out back
they'll be lined around the corner
come payday
for although she's good looking
it's the taste of her cooking
that keeps that steel line moving
through friday

almind

sunblocked sky sweats
where it meets my skin
warming to rainfall
sky drinks me in

☙

in the way is still involved

a nest in winter

a little is all i ever want
what varies is how often
i may be out of your loop
but i continue to be loopy
check your straight lines friends ... they're unnatural, and fear-based
to be loved
creative
generous
useful
trade any day of life
procurable – antisickenacow
a real person
in mythological worlds
and vice versa
stock dream footage
feeder fish think my feet are fish
ideomotor actor
i start holding my breath
the moment i feel it
although it is often
clear and steady breathing
that makes me available
for love in the first place

rise

        change
     vision
          capture
   release
teetering the fulcrum
      deceased undeceased

World Of If

Wierd, sci-fi Zen. The oddball art of Boyd McPeek is paired with the off-kilter poetry of Charles Luden. Scurfpea Publishing became aware of a collection of Luden's shorter poems and another of McPeek's art. OK, one of our editors saw Boyd doodling in a coffee shop and had always been a fan of Luden's work. He paired their material and showed it to them. Everyone was surprised at the result. Sometimes the whole IS greater than the sum of the parts. This book can't be described. Check inside it at *www.scurfpeapublishing.com* or at *www.amazon.com*.

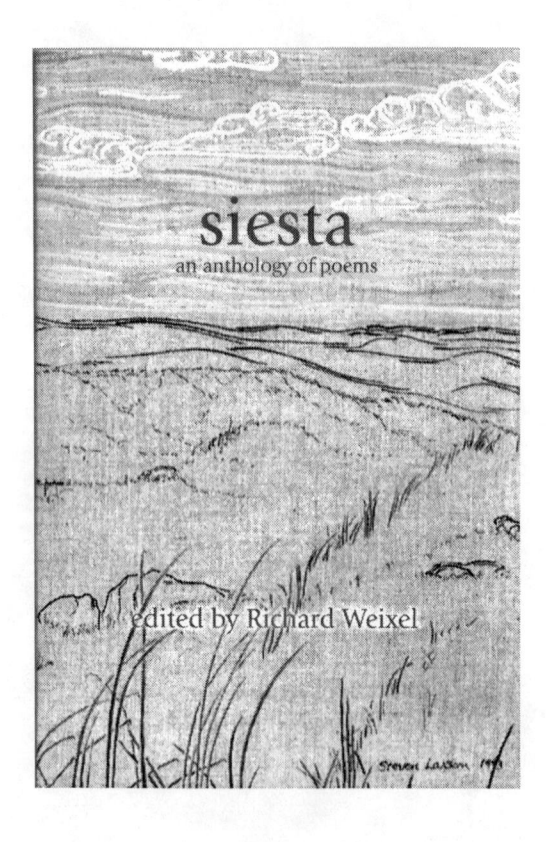

siesta

Poems by Bruce Roseland (whose previous books won the 2007 Wrangler Award for Outstanding Book of Poetry and the 2009 Will Rogers Medallion), Mary O'Connor (who has had residencies in both the MacDowell Colony and Ragdale and whose work has won awards from the Academy of American Poets), and 16 other excellent poets including Raybo.